Buying Your First Home

What You Need to Do

BY:

James Stevens

Published by Shepal Publishing

Table of Contents

Introduction

Buying your first home should be a thrilling experience, and an amazing accomplishment. Many people desire to own their homes, though they may not have the courage or the know how to get started. If you have made up your mind to be a home owner, congratulations! You are about to make a major investment, and to do so, you require all the information possible so that you do not make the wrong decision.

Before you make your final decision when buying your first home, you need the right guidance to help you avoid expensive mistakes. There are many angles to be aware of when making an investment, as well as information to help you cover all your bases. You need to familiarize yourself with all of these before you finalize your venture to purchase your first home.

This eBook is an excellent tool for all first time home buyers. With it, you will have all the facts that you need at your fingertips, and you can start looking for the home of your dreams.

Chapter 1:
The Basics of Buying a Home

Rent values are increasing, living within the city is becoming exceptionally expensive, and anyone seeking independence will find it challenging to live with relatives for extended periods. These are some of the reasons that more people are seeking to become home owners. As your home is likely to be the most expensive purchase you will ever make, you need to know the basics so that you will get what you expect while you are searching.

When you actually start looking for your first home, you are bound to experience mixed emotions. These would include excitement, confusion and even stress, as you may not know where you should start and what you need to expect. The basics that you should keep in mind when considering the purchase of your first home are as follows: -

Research Extensively

When purchasing your home, do not make a hurried choice or finalize after looking at only a few properties. You need to be comfortable with your purchase for the long term. Before you research, define what your needs are as well as your wants, so that as you search you can determine whether the property available is the right choice. You can get a better idea of what is available by visiting some of the homes that are on sale in the area that you want to make a purchase.

There are several factors that you should think about when making your decision, to help you eliminate what you do not want. These include considering the number of bedrooms in the home, the number of bathrooms and their locations, your preferred living area and whether a dining room is important, outdoor seating and space, neighbors and so on. The more extensive your list, the better it will be for you to narrow down your search so that you are only looking at properties that meet your criteria. This will save you time and energy.

Be Guided by your Budget

You need a realistic budget that you will use when buying your first home. You should look for a home that you can afford. Your financial source may be accumulated savings or you may be choosing to get a loan or mortgage for the value of the home. When you are seeking outside financing, take note of the interest rates that you will have to pay over time, and the number of years you will be paying back the mortgage.

Also take note that when paying for your first home, your expenses extend beyond the price of the home you are purchasing. There are some additional transaction costs that need to be factored in as well, and these will vary based on the home that you want to buy.

Factor in future costs within your budget, such as those that you pay for taxes as well as insurance in the years to come. Furthermore, you will have some maintenance costs to consider, especially if you are hoping to sell your home again in the future so that you can upgrade.

Choose your Preferred Home Type

There are different types of homes and you should know exactly what you want to buy for your first purchase. Some of the available types include condos, single family homes, duplexes, town houses, ranch, split-level, apartments, semi-detached homes, bungalows and so on. As you make your decision, consider whether you want to have a yard or not, and whether the costs of maintenance are affordable.

Here is what you can expect from different home types. Condos are perfectly maintained for you, with all expenses paid therefore if you are looking for a home that will cost less in terms of maintenance, this could be a perfect choice. Should there be any additional charges for services, these are often quite minimal.

A duplex gives you the freedom of renting your space to another dweller, for income purposes, or to help you pay off a mortgage. This can help make your home much more affordable and ensure that you go through the process with less stress.

Ranch homes allow for flexibility, as there are a number of rooms found in the U shaped or L shaped home that are all interchangeable. This means that should you have purchased a family home, and your children grow and leave the nest, you can transform a bedroom into a home office or a hobby space. They are typically on one floor and open in nature.

Bungalows are excellent for privacy, and for having your own garden and outdoor space. In a bungalow, you also enjoy security while being close enough to your neighbors that you can benefit from their help when you need it. They are highly popular amongst people of varying social classes because they have the appeal of being affordable, and are also able to fit into the dream of someone who has a bigger budget due to the range of styles available.

If you are looking for a unique style, then you could choose a split level home. This is a home which has a range of floor elevations. It is perfect for building on a slope as it has the ability to naturally fit in with the landscape.

There are also styles of homes that you can consider, such as the cape cod home, Country French Style Homes, Colonial Homes and Victorian Homes.

Cape Cod homes are normally one to one and a half story homes with steep roofs and windows which have multiple panes which are designed to let in as much light as is possible.

Colonial Homes are large, featuring two to three story's, wood facades with brick, and internally, large fireplaces in several rooms. The bedrooms are often on the second floor, while the living room and kitchen are located on the first floor.

Country French Style Homes feature sloppy roofs and narrow windows, and they have elements of timber that have been built into the frame.

Romantic looking homes typically fall within the Victorian style, which can be old fashioned with rich texture and color, or more contemporary built from modern materials.

These are some of the more popular styles for homes, and the more you look at what is available, the easier it will become for you to decide on a design or elements that you would love for your first home.

Determine your preferred location

Where exactly do you want to buy a home? This is an important point to consider even before you get down to the actual plan. Everyone has a preferred location that they have been dreaming about for a long time. Your location should be based on other attributes, including whether the amenities you prefer are available, such as social amenities. Choose a location where you are close to some of your loved ones, your family or friends.

The location will also be determined by the amount of money you will be spending on the home. You need to be realistic on this as well, before you spot a house in a location that you cannot afford which could put a damper on your dreams. A home purchase is a big deal, so the location should be pleasing for you, and if you wish to upgrade in the future, it is best to look for a location where the properties turn excellent resale values as well.

Chapter 2:
Factors to Consider Before
Buying a Home

If you have a dream of owning a home, you should pursue that dream until you attain it. There are obstacles that you will face, and you need to know about them so that you can overcome them all. Doing so will help you make a decision that will please you for years to come. Below are some of the things that you might have to put into consideration before you make your first home purchase:

1. The state of the real estate market

When buying a home, you need to determine if the market is in favor of the buyer or the seller. This will give you an idea of how much money you will be paying for the home and how easy it will be to find the home of your dreams. The most ideal time to buy a home is when it is the buyer's market. This means that there will be a large number of homes that are up for sale at that time in the market and only a few buyers willing to buy the homes. This interprets to having many homes at an affordable price for the few buyers that are willing to buy. It is recommended to use the services of a local real estate agent for more accurate market speculation. This will prevent you from overspending which can affect the value of your home for you.

2. The process of buying a home

A home purchase is totally different from any other kind of purchase that people make because of the process that is involved. You will need a lot of paper work which you may not understand a thing about. There is a lot that you need to learn way before the actual purchase so as to avoid making costly mistakes. Some of the steps you should not miss out on during the process of purchase include saving enough money for down payment, house inspection, expenses like repairs if any would be needed, upgrades, closing costs among others. You also need to ensure that you will have enough money for the monthly payments of the mortgage if you are using this medium to make your purchase.

3. The Home Evaluation

When you have selected a home that you consider worth buying, take time to check it out. This will require you to visit the home and look around, trying to identify what could be wrong with it. Can you see any mold? How thick are the walls? Are there any pests lurking in cupboards? Check everything. This will help you establish what within the house will need to be repaired before you move in, and also, how much you are willing to spend to get these repairs done. If the work to be done is extensive, you may even be able to negotiate for a discount on the price so that you get a better deal.

4. Pressure

How stable is your job? Do you think you will have your job in years to come should you apply for a mortgage? These are factors that you must think about when looking to purchase your first home. Once you start on the journey, you should follow through to the end as failure to do so, could cost you the dream home that you are aspiring towards. While you consider this, also ensure that the decision that you make is based on the income that you are earning now, and not what you may possibly be earning in the future.

In addition, you will find that there are many people who may put pressure on you to complete the process to purchase. This may be because they are going to get a commission, or someone believes that you are getting a good deal. If for any reason you are not comfortable with the purchase, take some time to think about it before you finally commit. Do not let anyone push you or force you into a decision. Stay in control as in the end, it is your investment to make and you do not want to have any regrets.

Chapter 3:
Getting Your Money in Order

The success of any investment depends on the amount of money that you are willing to put in that investment, which is why you need to plan for your finances and put them in order before you can start thinking of buying your first home. As this is your first home, there is an 80% possibility that you will need financial assistance through a mortgage to purchase this home. If you have somehow managed to accumulate the amount required through savings, or perhaps someone left you a large inheritance, they the process and the decision that you make in the end can be much easier. Otherwise, here are some things that you need to have in order: -

Your credit score. This is very important whenever you are applying for a mortgage. The higher your credit score, the better interest rate you get for any mortgage. A small difference in the interest rate can save you thousands of dollars in the long run, which is why you should do what it takes to get the most affordable mortgage you can get for your home purchase. Clear your debts and ensure that all your bills are paid on time. Maintain a good record for as long as possible. This is the only way your credit score will look good in the eyes of the lenders. A good score gives you the power to negotiate better terms.

Find out how much money you qualify for should you want a mortgage. You need a home loan lender to **pre-approve you for a mortgage**. With this knowledge, you will know how much you can afford to pay in mortgage installments each month, which will help you decide what type of home would be best for you to buy. Getting pre-approved for a mortgage works in favor of a home buyer in more than one way; you can now confidently contact a real estate agent to start the search for a home of your dreams. Sellers find it easy to deal with buyers who have already been pre-approved for a mortgage because they are sure that the deal will eventually go through if the buyer loves the home that the seller is selling.

Shopping for a mortgage

This should be done before you start looking for a home. Many people will not understand this at first but you need to know about the money so that you will know the kind of home that you will afford with that amount of money. Save yourself from high expectations and dashed hopes by doing this the other way around. This way, you will avoid the frustration of having a good home in mind that you cannot afford to pay for.

Shopping for a mortgage will also prepare you on the amount of down payment that you will make for the house. Do not assume that all sellers are the same and will give you fixed terms. Sellers will want to know how much money you will be willing to pay as down payment for the house, and the rest of the money will be covered by the mortgage. If you do not have this information available for them, then any offer that you make on the property that you want could be ignored.

You also need to know the ratios that the mortgage lenders that you have considered are using to issue out their mortgages. This should be in line with the budget that you came up with in the beginning. If for instance you are able to part with 38% of your monthly income to cater for the mortgage expenses, you should go for a mortgage that fits in that percentage. These ratios also determine if you will qualify for the mortgage or not, because if the remaining percentage of your monthly income is not sufficient to cater for the outstanding debts then you will not be able to pay back the mortgage.

Once you are sure that you qualify for the mortgage, you can now proceed to check out the programs that best suits a first time home buyer like you. There are so many such programs in the real estate market and they are designed to help first time home buyers make excellent and informed choices.

Chapter 4:
Shopping for a Home of Your Dreams

With your finances sorted out, the picture in your mind crystal clear, and your head and heart full of motivation, you are ready to take the next step and start shopping for the home of your dreams. Unlike a grocery store, you cannot simply walk in, make your selection from a choice of similar products, and walk out in seconds. Shopping for the home of your dreams needs you to take time and consideration, so that you can find something that is perfect for all your needs. Here are some of the actions that you need to take in the process.

Use a Realtor

It will help you to find a professional and highly qualified real estate agent or representative to help you with the search and the negotiations for your first home. The kind of agent that you will pick for this job should have several key attributes including being well experienced in real estate matters, open minded, interesting to deal with, confident and fully qualified as a real estate agent. If possible, they should be registered with a body that governs the field, as additional proof that they know what they are doing. Below are some of the factors you will consider when choosing a real estate agent:

1. Their rates: What they charge for their services should matter as this will determine your cost at the end of the purchase. Your best bet is to find a realtor who charges you a percentage of the sale price as is standard in the industry, as following any other rating system could lead to you being exploited. At least with the

percentage, you know what you will be paying no matter which home you choose to buy in the end.

2. Methods: Understand the methods that your preferred real estate agent uses to search and purchase homes and choose a realtor that uses methods agreeable with you.

3. Experience: How long the realtor has been in the market should matter as experienced ones can get you better homes faster than the inexperienced ones. They will also be able to advice you well since experience comes with great knowledge pertaining to the real estate market.

4. Training: Is your realtor trained? What level of training has he received? Since you will be dealing with a large amount of money, you need to be sure that the person who is handling the transaction knows all the terminology, and can identify a loop hole with their knowledge.

The realtor of your choice should live in the locality where you are interested in buying your first home. This way, he will know where to look to get you the house of your dreams based on any criteria you provide. The realtor will be familiar with the procedure of buying a home in that location too, and this will speed up things for you.

He should be one that works full time to ensure that nothing delays the process of you finalizing your home purchase. A part time realtor will also not have enough time to exhaust the search in order to get you a perfect home.

You also need to get a realtor that has a reputation of closing many deals in a year. This is how you know if yours will be a successful deal or not. Bear in mind that not all deals go through to the end, therefore choose a realtor wisely to increase your chances of closing the deal.

Once you get a good realtor, take time to explain to him just what you want your first home to be. You need to exhaust all the details so as to give him most of the things he needs to consider when searching for your home. Go into specific details about the number of bedrooms you want in your home for instance, the number and kind of bathrooms, the finishing, if you need a home with its own garden or not among so many other details. Anything that you have in your mind should be told to the realtor since he is the one out there representing your needs.

Use an alert service

There are alert services that can help you learn about available properties within the area of your preference. You only subscribe to get alerts about properties within that specific area that falls within your price range. This way, you can compare and choose one that best fits your preferred home description.

Physically look for a home within your budget

Since you already have a budget in mind and you know how much money you want to spend on your first home, you can start the physical search on your own. Other people close to you for instance your friends and relatives can help in the search as well. The challenge many people face is in determining their range. Financial advisors will tell you to ensure that you are not paying more than 38% of your income in a month on home expenses, which includes the monthly mortgage instalment payments and other debts you may be in for the sake of your home purchase. When coming up with a budget, ensure that it fits perfectly within your income so as to be sure that you will not default the mortgage, which could lead to a lost investment.

Visit a few homes that are on sale

Sometimes one does not have an idea of what exactly they want until they physically see a home, then they start thinking of how good it would be if they had some things in their homes. By visiting a home on sale, you will see what is in the market, then you will be able to make decisions on what you want in your first home.

Do not visit just a few homes in one area but homes in a different area as well, then compare the two. This is how you end up making the right choices.

Chapter 5:
Making an Offer on a Home

When buying a home, you will pay a considerable amount of attention to the price of the home. However, this is not the most crucial factor. Both the price and the terms of purchase should be considered when one is making an offer for a home that they are eying. This is because the terms of buying determine the total amount of money that you will be paying for the home. Terms of purchase in most cases represent a good amount of money in excess of the actual value of the home and this is an additional cost that home buyers should always be aware of. The terms of buying are therefore very important and they should be reviewed in detail by the buyer before he can go for any offer.

How much money is involved?

The amount of money that a buyer should offer for a certain home is typically a percentage which is below the seller's asking price. This should be an amount of money that is less than what you are actually willing to pay for the home. The offer price is always dependent on the basic laws that govern supply and demand of homes in a certain location. According to these laws, if there is a high demand for homes in a certain location, the seller will most likely get full price or even more for the home as an offer. If the demand is low, the opposite happens, therefore the seller can expect to get a price that is way below the asking price.

How to make an offer

Different procedures are involved when one is making an offer for a certain home in different places across the country. In most cases, the home buyer will be required to complete an offer sheet document that will be issued by the realtor. This will be given to the owner of the home or the seller thereafter. After this the home owner can accept or reject the offer depending on what offer the buyer has presented, or he can make a counter offer, which has to be agreed upon by the buyer.

The offer that the buyer initially makes remains the binding sales contract if it will be accepted by the home owner. This is also what will be used as the purchase agreement. That is why such offers are required to have all the elements that will be needed in a blueprint for the final sale agreement. Such an offer should have:

1. The address and description of the property in question.

2. The selling price.

3. The terms of sale- here you will state whether you will be paying the property in cash or you will get a mortgage loan for the purchase.

4. A promissory note by the seller that he will provide full ownership of the property and the kind of title deed he will give the buyer.

5. The actual sale date.

6. The method through which the real estate taxes will be settled between the buyer and the seller. These includes water bills, fuels, taxes, rents, utilities among others.

7. The amount of money that you are giving with the offer, which is the very first deposit you will make for the home purchase. State whether it is in cash, as a promise or in check form. State how the money should be sent back to you in case the offer is rejected.

8. A provision about who will pay for the home inspections that will be conducted between the buyer and he seller.

Counter offers are very common during home purchases. Any changes that a seller makes on the offer the buyer sends to him is always considered as a counter offer. That is why the negotiation process is considered very important to the buyer, because everything is agreed upon during this period of home purchase. The buyer should be very close to the realtor so as to know the progress of the negotiations and also to agree on the change that the seller has made on the initial offer.

Home inspections

Inspections are very important in any home purchase because they ensure that everything is okay before the buyer finally signs the deal. There are different kinds of inspections that are conducted in real estate purchases especially when it involves home buying. There are check on termites for instance, surveys that are conducted on borderlines, appraisals that will determine the value of different home loan lenders, reviews and also structural inspections. Structural inspections are very important at this stage.

During these kinds of inspections, an inspector will be required to pay a visit to the property in order to check if there are any physical defects in the property and also in the material used in its construction. The inspector will provide a report that will show if there will be any need for expensive repairs and replacements in the few yeas that will come. The inspector can take between 3-5 hours depending on how big the home is. A buyer is required to attend such inspections to see for himself the kind of property that he will be paying for. He will be given a chance to ask any questions he might have on the mechanics and the structure of the property if he will have any. It is also an opportunity for the home buyers to learn a thing or two more about the home of their interest.

Chapter 6:
Home Insurance

Even though the law is not very strict on this, there is no sensible home owner that should be without an insurance for their home. The main benefit of home insurance is to protect the home owner against any loss in case of a catastrophe. In case something bad ever happens to your home, you can be assured that the insurance company will take the risk, and you will not be counting any losses. That is why insuring your home is very important. This is particularly important for new home owners because it often gets 'swept under the carpet' since the new home is not expected to have any issues.

When to insure

The right time for a home buyer to get a home insurance policy and also a warranty for their home is at closing. You need to speak to your realtor before the closing in order to let him know what exactly you need. He should be able to give you all the details that will be required for the cover. Some of the things you can ask from him are issues pertaining to costs, limitations endorsements, deductibles among others.

The kind of insurance to choose

Home owners need to know that there are so many different forms of insurance covers that are associated with home ownership. These are all worth considering if they want to insure their homes. The major types of covers you can choose from include the following:

a) The title insurance: This is the kind of insurance that protects home owners in case the title of the property they have already bought is found to be invalid. If this was to happen, the home buyer will lose any mortgage loan as well as the down payment that has been made for the home. With this insurance cover, you will be required to make a onetime payment at closing. The coverage will include the loan lenders policies, which will offer protection up to the mortgage amount of the property. There is also the owner's coverage that will protect the owners purchase price.

b) Flood Insurance: This is necessary in areas that are prone to floods. This cover is offered mainly by the government in order to protect home owners against losses associated with floods. It is important to talk to your realtor in order to determine if you really need this cover especially if you will be buying a home that is close to a riparian area.

c) Homeowners insurance: This is the insurance cover that protects the home owner against any kind of loss that he may face in his home. The cover provides fire, theft and liability coverage and it aims at protecting any valuable item that the home owner might have in that house. Some of the items protected through this cover can be furniture, home office equipment, and valuable items like wedding rings among others.

Things to Keep in Mind

You might need a contact person at a reputable insurance company or even an agent who is well qualified and also authorized to offer advice and help in insuring your home.

Most of the agents that you will get only represent one single insurance company and these may not offer the right kind of help and support to help you make the best choice. Check if you will get an independent agent or broker that represents different insurance companies to get the best advice from him.

Do not under insure your home. Anything can happen to your home any time and the loss can be great. You do not want a situation where you are not receiving compensation because you under insured your home. When talking to insurance brokers, specify that you want to insure your home properly. Many will not be quick to tell you how much money you will need to insure the entire home because it is expensive, that is why home owners end up under-insuring their homes. Work with the actual cost of insuring the entire home and everything in it and compare for better rates.

Be as truthful as possible when you are insuring your home. This way, the insurance company will know the actual size of your home, its style of construction, improvements if any, features, any special features, structures and anything else that will matter to the insurance.

Always report any major improvements that you make on your home to the insurance company as this is important for the insurance cover.

You should work hard to get a good but affordable cover at all times. Insurance companies charge different rates for their home insurance policies. You should shop far and wide to ensure that you are paying less for the best cover.

Home warranties

New homes these days come with warranties. After a builder is done with a new home, he makes himself available so that in case of a need for any repairs, he will be there to do the work. However there are some instances the builder is not available and in such a case, the new home owner will be required to pay for the repairs, which can be very costly. This is why a home warranty is necessary because it offers protection to home owners. The warranty comes with certain benefits that a new home owner may be interested in, for instance workmanship for a period of up to one year and also mechanical benefits like plumbing and wiring for up to two years. Warranties for existing homes differ a little from those for the new homes. The warranties are provided by the sellers and in case of a need, the warranty company will come to provide the needed help and services.

Chapter 7:
Important Home Buying Tips
to Keep in Mind

Thus far, you have gone through all the information you need to help you make a wise and informed decision. You have an idea about the different types of houses that are available, and the styles that you can find with these houses. You also know when would be the best time to purchase a house, and how you should look. Yet, there are still some pointers that you need to help make the entire process easier. This section features all the tips that you need to keep in mind.

1. Determine how much money you can afford

Everyone would love to pick out a perfect home that they would want to own but we are always limited by finances. It can be very frustrating if you have already set your eyes on a certain home, only to realize that you cannot afford it. That is why you need to know just how much money you can raise for your dream home. Do not look at how much you earn every month but at how much money is left once you take out all your expenditure for that month. This will let you know whether you will be able to afford a meal once you sign on the dotted line and purchase your house.

2. Take some time to learn from the experts

Learning from the experts is always the best way to get started. A mistake made during the first home purchase could come to haunt you in the future and you may not get to make such an investment once again. That is why it is important to first of all take some time and learn as much as you can. If there is a seminar for first time home buyers that you can attend, do so by all means. They are organized all the time by a good number of organizations and experts in home buying come in order to give new buyers some useful tips that can help them in making a successful first purchase. You even get to learn how to maintain your home once you buy it as well, in order to enjoy it for a while longer.

3. Take note of what you want and what you need

If you want to be happy with your first home purchase, your needs and wants have to be well considered. Come up with a list of things that you want in that home and its surroundings, prioritizing the things that you may not do without. Include things that you have always wanted to have in your home and ensure that you are listing the kinds of social amenities that you want to be close to and the distance you prefer to live from town or from the nearest mall. This way, you will be able to narrow down your options to a home that will at least make you happy even if you will not get all the needs and wants in one home.

Then there are the things that you need, which if they are not in the home, the sale would not be worth it. You should be clear about these as well to avoid future regret.

4. Choose the Right Area

An area that is up and coming is the best place that a first time home buyer can seek out a property. These are lower in price, and are often newly constructed. If you are purchasing a house that is not new, then the damages that are on the house should be minimal which will save your repair costs.

In addition, no matter where you home is located, it is unlikely that you will find a home that has been fantastically maintained when you are making a purchase. They will almost always need some work or renovations done to bring them up to par. Accept this, and understand that finding a house that ticks 100% of your boxes will be difficult. If you can find at least 80%, then you are getting a great deal.

Finally, in relation to the area, the population is also important. Should you be looking at purchasing an apartment, if there are a high percentage of tenants in the building, then it is unlikely that the building will be well maintained and taken care of, as the sheer volume of people may make this an uphill task. Therefore, you should avoid an investment of this nature. You would do better looking for an area that has a lower population, no matter what type of home that you are purchasing. Lower populations mean there are less strains that are placed on the infrastructure, so you will be able to enjoy services much faster. Furthermore, you are less likely to end up in a dispute with those who live close to you as there will be enough of everything to go around.

Chapter 8:
First-Time Home Buying Mistakes To Watch Out For

First time home buyers are usually very excited when shopping for a new home. In as much as the entire experience can be scary and sometimes exhausting, the excitement is always there and this is the reason why so many mistakes are made. Many first time home buyers already know what they are looking for, which is a home that they will love and also a home that they can easily afford, but the whole process becomes overwhelming.

Even with the best plan in place and when things seem easy flowing, mistakes are likely to occur and these are the mistakes that makes it impossible for one to end up with a home of their dreams. One thing that home buyers should know is that every mistake that they make in such a purchase is costly, therefore you might end up paying more money than you intended if you are not careful enough. Some of the common costly mistakes first time home buyers make are:

Skipping the mortgage qualification step

This is a very important stage in the home buying process for the home buyers that will need a mortgage loan to finance their purchase. Most of the time, what a buyer thinks he can afford is not what the bank is willing to offer as a mortgage loan. Sometimes one may qualify for so much less, and if you have already signed the contract, you might end up frustrated, wasting much of your time, the seller's time and the time for everyone else that was involved in the purchase. That is why getting a pre-approval for a loan is very important so that you will know how much you can afford beforehand then you can proceed to sign the contracts.

People with an unstable income and those that have a poor credit score can only qualify for a small amount of money as loan, and this may not be your plan. If you know this early enough, you can work to repair your credit rating in order to qualify for a higher amount of money, then you will be able to sign the contract knowing that you will meet the end of your bargain in the purchase.

Being easily swept away

Home sellers will use all kinds of tricks in order to ensure that they are selling their homes as fast as possible and at a higher cost. These tricks work on many buyers and before they know it, they have already signed the contract and are already paying for a home that is different from what they actually wanted. A seller will for instance use some minor upgrades on a home in order to charge a higher price for it, even if the upgrade did not cost him so much. Some sellers use cosmetic fixes in order to get more money from home buyers. These tricks will make you pay more than you were planning to spend on a home if you are not careful enough.

If you are working with a budget, it is important to stick to it to the end. Financial advisers will tell you to invest in a home that you can add value to, so as to avoid paying more on the purchase and also to give your home a higher value once you have already bought it.

Ignoring the additional expenses

Home buyers should always be prepared for the additional expenses that they will have to incur after the home purchase. Other than servicing your loan, there are a host of other expenses that are linked to the process, which you only discover once they crop up. Such expenses include property taxes, insurance, any repairs and replacements that will be needed in your home among others.

These have to be planned for whenever you are planning to take up a loan so that you will plan for some money that will be used to cater for all the expenses. In some cases some home owners are required to pay a certain amount of money as maintenance charges every month especially those who own condos. You should budget for these well to minimize surprises afterwards when the time to pay for them will come.

Not thinking about the future

This is a very important thing before you finally settle on a certain location. Many people ignore this aspect in the home buying process because it is not very easy to tell how a certain neighborhood can be in the future. However, so much information is online these days and you can use the information provided on the location you have chosen to buy your home as a basis to try to imagine how the future will be. If it is a fast growing location for instance, you can imagine how it will be in just a few years, then you can determine if this is the kind of location you want to live in or not.

Sometimes people are faced with unpleasant surprises after buying a home because they did not investigate the locating really well and this makes it hard for them to settle in their new home. To avoid making this mistake, research far and wide about the location and how people think about its future, then you will make a wise decision thereafter. Some of the guiding factors you can take into consideration are:

o The kind of developmental plans that are underway in that neighborhood.

o The kinds of buildings that could come up in the future if there is some undeveloped land in the location.

o The kind of street your street will be in the future, a major or a popular street.

o How the value of homes in the neighborhood has been changing.

o The zoning laws in the area of your choice.

Overlooking the most important things

First time home buyers are usually well prepared to buy a home of their dream but little things happen in the process and they tend to forget the most important things. A person who was looking for a three bedroomed house for instance because he is planning to have children may end up buying a two bedroom house. This is a regrettable and a very costly mistake. One of the things that makes people compromise on the most important things is the cost. A person who wants a home of his own in order to enjoy his peace and quiet with his family might end up with a condo just because it is cheaper. What happens is that you do not get to enjoy the most important things that made you buy a home in the first place and you might not be happy with the purchase for a very long time.

Conclusion

Buying your first home need not be a confusing affair; you can enjoy the entire process and enjoy the home that you eventually buy for so many years to come. This however is only possible if you go through each step of the process with a lot of care. You need to start by knowing what to expect and what to do as well as the right decisions to make for every step. This guide has information that can guide you on what to do until you finally pick out the home that you are interested in.

Do not rush to make a bid though, even when you are overwhelmed by excitement and you cannot wait to make the home your own. Compare other homes similar to the one that you are about to buy, especially those in the same location as your chosen home. Check out what other home buyers paid for their homes and what their first payment was. If the buyers were able to buy their homes at about 5% below the asking price, negotiate for price reduction too and prepare to pay at least lower than that, maybe 8 or 10% lower than the asking price. This will help you to reduce your cost by a huge percentage.

Always work hand in hand with your real estate agent and ensure that he is doing everything for your own interest. You are paying for his services after all, and the least he can do is to make sure that you are satisfied with the way he is serving you.

If you are able to follow though this guide, be assured of a happy and easy first time home buying experience.

www.ingramcontent.com/pod-product-compliance
Lightning Source LLC
Chambersburg PA
CBHW070424190526
45169CB00003B/1404